Tiny Confessions

Tiny Confessions

The Secret Thoughts
of Dogs, Cats, and Everything

Christopher Rozzi

A PERIGEE BOOK

A PERIGEE BOOK
Published by the Penguin Group
Penguin Group (USA) Inc.
375 Hudson Street, New York, New York 10014, USA

USA I Canada I UK I Ireland I Australia I New Zealand I India I South Africa I China

Penguin Books Ltd., Registered Offices: 80 Strand, London WC2R 0RL, England
For more information about the Penguin Group, visit penguin.com.

TINY CONFESSIONS

ISBN: 978-0-399-16106-3

First edition: May 2013

PRINTED IN THE UNITED STATES OF AMERICA

10 9 8 7 6 5 4 3 2

While the author has made every effort to provide accurate telephone numbers,
Internet addresses, and other contact information at the time of publication, neither
the publisher nor the author assumes any responsibility for errors, or for changes that
occur after publication. Further, the publisher does not have any control over and does
not assume any responsibility for author or third-party websites or their content.

Most Perigee books are available at special quantity discounts for bulk purchases for
sales promotions, premiums, fund-raising, or educational use. Special books, or book
excerpts, can also be created to fit specific needs. For details, write: Special Markets,
Penguin Group (USA) Inc., 375 Hudson Street, New York, New York 10014.

To Mom and Dad,
for giving me everything I needed to be creative,
and then letting my mind wander a little.

I forgot where I buried that thing that you loved.

I would like to find a happy medium between wrestling and napping.

Anywhere I lie down is extremely comfortable.

I could literally
spend an entire
day just pushing
your phone off
a table.

I believe I will be a great hunter, once my legs grow in fully.

When I see anyone else on your lap, I feel betrayed.

I sometimes dream
that I'm walking
a smaller version of you.

I momentarily
fall in love
with everything
I rub up
against.

When I wreak havoc,
I feel what I believe to be
an emotion.

I have begun the lengthy process of judging your new friend.

When I look at you, I see a giant, walking treat.

I share in your attraction
to Matthew McConaughey.

I wish I had more of a say in my own physical appearance.

I yearn to develop a less intrusive way to say "hello."

Sometimes I feel like I am the human and you are the instinct-driven animal.

I would probably even befriend your enemies.

I'm troubled by my lack of any long-term goals.

I believe that my endless
stamina derives from these
magical energy spots.

I hope you understood what I was trying to say when I ate the couch.

I am a surprisingly
complex tapestry of
feelings and emotions.

I have no concept of how small I am.

My friends and I like to pretend we're the ladies of "The View."

I view each distraction as an opportunity to reevaluate my existence.

To procure food items at parties,
I linger near pushovers.

Surprisingly, I don't enjoy being compared to science fiction characters.

I often have no idea
what I am laughing about.

I worry that our new video
will not be as popular as the last.

I am beginning to think
you don't understand
my snort language.

This is my
happy face.

I absolutely adore you;
all others are on notice.

I hope to one day
capture the red light.

I feel no shame
in trading etiquette
for food.

I would probably sing
if you ordered me to.

I do not apply logic to any aspect of my life.

I am admittedly liberal
in terms of smooch distribution.

I'd like to corral everyone in the world into one room.

I exist in a constant state
of possibly unwarranted
celebration.

I have ingested items that some would refer to as "non-food."

I am concerned
about my own
unstable behavior.

While you were out,
I read that naughty book
on your night table.

Instead of barking,
I stare into your soul.

I would prefer it if you would not call me by my nicknames in public.

What you see as dancing is just me desperately scrambling to earn ham.

When you hold me
up to your ear,
I can hear your
house.

I am often bewildered by my own snorts.

I have attempted to end
several of your relationships.

I am not as promiscuous as some have suggested

I really hope you weren't
planning on wearing
that ever again.

I enjoy being pampered
to the point of near
exhaustion.

I would probably follow you into a volcano.

I love how excited you get
when I behave like you.

I am attempting to balance being both family-friendly yet wildly troubling toward bad people.

I have decided that every command calls for me to run around aimlessly.

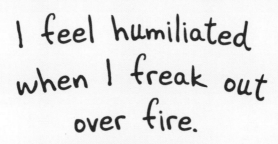

I feel humiliated
when I freak out
over fire.

I am unsure which end
the sounds I create
are emanating from.

I am completely
comfortable with
my appearance.

I secretly root against your sports teams.

I wish that I could
lie on your lap without
seriously hurting you.

I bring you this
mutilated doll
in order to say
"Welcome to
our home."

I was just trying to impress my mother.

Even I am slightly
repulsed by this ball
that I am offering you.

I feel I am unfairly
judged based solely on
looks and personality.

I find any comparison
to the waitstaff
wildly inappropriate.

If I were you, I would consider obtaining a restraining order against me.

My primary goal in life
is to have my
buttocks rubbed.

I have been working for the Department of Motor Vehicles since 1957.

When you're not around,
I laugh my head off
at that voice you do.

I am more delicate than my height and weight may suggest.

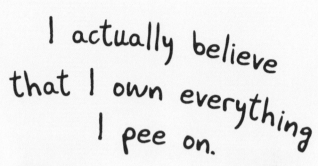

I actually believe
that I own everything
I pee on.

I enjoy being in situations that require leaping.

That mess I made is my way of thanking you for my awesome name.

I harbor resentment toward my own tail for divulging my inner excitement.

I sometimes fear
my snoring makes me
seem less ladylike.

I wish
I knew
my own
future.

When I bark
like crazy,
I'm trying to
tell you that
you're amazing.

I have information pertaining
to the whereabouts
of your shoe.

I do not
share your
insecurities.

I secretly long for the strong yet tender touch of a man.

I am hoping that
you will eventually just
sleep on the floor.

I'm actually a guy
in a costume.

I have seen my
own reflection and
I do not understand.

ACKNOWLEDGMENTS

For their help, both great and small:

Marian Lizzi, to whom I will be forever grateful for approaching me to do this book. Lauren Becker and everyone at Perigee for their hard work. Kari Stuart at ICM for her constant support. Rosalind Lichter, Esq., for keeping it legal. Anastasia Bonice Chung for introducing me to Fab.com. ZeroBoy for help with the first big sale. Matt Baer, Riian McCormick, and everyone at Fab.com. Everyone at Etsy.com. Stan Wolkoff at Masterpiece Printers. Nicole and Michael Chanin, David Baron, Kristine Tenace, Jennifer O'Keefe, and Gail Courtney for being my "text focus group." Honey Gorenberg for her Shelter Island retreats. Eugen Beer, Barbara McMahon, and Bones at Cool Culinaria for their constant help and support. The American Kennel Club. Jacqueline Stahl for always keeping me on track. I'd like to thank all of my family, friends, and fans around the world for their love and support throughout this process. Special thanks to Rebekkah Ross for saying "You should do paintings of dogs and cats . . ."

For resource images of their beautiful pets:

Dave Stangle; Angela Kissell; Kika; Liesl Apgar; Mike Hagen and Kathy Monahan; Amelia Glissman; Lauren Mehnert Asnis; Nicole Delorey; Sal, Coleen, Olivia, and Melanie Rozzi; Erica Bielemeier Slezak; Jocelyn Songco; Kathy Huck; Denise Yu; Jim Dale; Elisa Gierasch; J. Martinez and Jaysali Border Collies; Rachel S.; Megan; Randi Kiedes Vallejo; Frank Campanella; Ambrose Martos and Florence Montmare; Melissa Fox; Jocelyn Songco; Jennifer O'Keefe; Dr. Rhonda R. Dodd; Frances Lachowicz; Kate Varner DiCesare and Darien Varner; David Gilligan; Todd and Elizabeth Drazien; Heather Sibley; Meredith Rush; Angie Manresa; Claire Hampshire; Erika D'Amato Negrin; Ashley Gioia; Gail Courtney; Marc Griffiths; Christopher Lee and Rebekkah Ross; and Suzy McQuown.

To our bichon, Willie: Thanks for making me curious about your inner monologue.

And finally my beautiful wife, Pauline, whose love, humor, and intelligence inspire everything that I do. Thanks for acting like a ridiculous child with me way more than we probably should.

ABOUT THE AUTHOR

Christopher Rozzi is a writer, artist, and comedian. When not conjuring up Tiny Confessions, Chris spends his time dressing in costume for his absurd one-man comedies, *Outré Island* and *Bezinkule*. Mr. Rozzi lives in New York City with his wife, Pauline Miller, and their bichon, Willie. His website is www.tinyconfessions.com.